Goodbye Tessa

by Elizabeth Dale and John Johnson

W

FRANKLIN WATTS

LONDON•SYDNEY

Leo and Tessa were best friends. They were always together. Every morning Tessa woke Leo up with a lick. Tessa had loved playing with Leo ever since she was a puppy. She always wanted to play ball with him.

One day, Leo's mum told him that Tessa was going to have puppies. Leo was thrilled. He took special care of Tessa.
When the puppies were born, Leo was the first to see them. He gazed at them in wonder.

Leo loved every single puppy, but his favourite was the smallest. Leo named him Jasper. Jasper looked just like Tessa and copied everything she did.

Jasper loved Leo, too. He gave Leo

lots of licks.

"Can we keep Tessa's puppies?" Leo asked.

"No," his mum laughed. "We haven't got

room for them all. Anyway, we've already

found homes for them."

One by one, the puppies went to new homes until Jasper was the only one left. Leo hoped that Jasper's new owner, Mrs Green, had changed her mind. Finally, she came to collect him. She was delighted when she saw the little puppy.

"I will have to take you for lots of walks," she said to Jasper. "You will keep me fit and be my best friend!"

Leo was sad to see Jasper leave, but he was glad his favourite little puppy had a nice owner and a lovely new home.

Leo was upset when Jasper had gone.

Tessa seemed to know. She took her ball to

Leo and dropped it at his feet, begging him

to play. Leo laughed. He picked it up and

threw it for her.

Leo and Tessa had fun all year long.

In summer, they went to the park every day.

But then, one day, Leo noticed that

Tessa wasn't running as fast as usual.

"What's wrong, Tessa?" said Leo.

Tessa flopped down at Leo's feet.

She looked up at him

and panted. Leo hugged her.

"Let's go home," he said.

9

The next morning, Tessa didn't come and wake

Leo up with a lick, as she usually did.

He rushed downstairs to hug her.

Tessa licked him, but she looked tired.

All day, Leo gave Tessa her favourite treats.

He cuddled her and told her he loved her.

"I think she might be ill," said his mum.

"Let's take her to see the vet."

The vet checked Tessa thoroughly. She took
some blood to test and listened to her heart.
"Tessa is just getting old," she said, sadly.
"The best thing for her now is lots of hugs."

Leo gave Tessa hugs all evening, and he reminded her of all the good times they'd had together. When he went to bed, Leo dreamt of happy times – playing with Tessa at the beach, and having fun in the park. He even dreamt that Tessa was a naughty puppy again, playing with his mum's slippers!

Sadly, Tessa died in the night. Leo's mum told him the bad news as soon as he woke up. "Tessa died peacefully in her basket," she said. "She had her ball beside her. I'm sure she was happy and not in any pain." Leo cried, he was so sad.

Leo and his mum buried Tessa with
her favourite ball underneath the apple tree.
Leo lay flowers on her grave. All week,
he went there every day after school.

One afternoon, Leo's mum came out to sit

with him.

"Would you like another dog one day –

a puppy to play with?" she asked him.

Leo shook his head. "I only want Tessa,"

he said, sadly.

As the weeks went by, Leo still missed Tessa, but he didn't feel quite as sad. Then one day, they had unexpected visitors – Mrs Green and Jasper! Leo and Jasper were delighted to see each other again. Everyone laughed when Jasper grabbed Leo's mum's slippers from under the chair, just like Tessa used to do!

Tessa's puppy reminded Leo so much of her. He hugged Jasper. Thinking of Tessa suddenly made Leo really happy again. They had had so many lovely times together.

Mrs Green was very sad to hear about Tessa.

She had sad news, too.

"I'm moving into a flat and I'm not allowed

pets," she said. "I will have to find Jasper

a new home. Do you know anyone

who wants a puppy?"

Suddenly, Leo knew just what to do.

"Jasper can live with us!" he said. "You can still

visit him here anytime you like, Mrs Green."

"That's very kind of you, Leo!" Mrs Green said.

Jasper licked Leo on the nose and everybody

laughed. It seemed that everyone agreed!

Story order

Look at these 5 pictures and captions.
Put the pictures in the right order
to retell the story.

1

Tessa is checked by the vet.

2

Leo visits Tessa's grave.

3

Leo gets to keep Jasper.

4

Tessa gets tired at the park.

5

Tessa has lots of puppies.

Independent Reading

This series is designed to provide an opportunity for your child to read on their own. These notes are written for you to help your child choose a book and to read it independently.

In school, your child's teacher will often be using reading books which have been banded to support the process of learning to read. Use the book band colour your child is reading in school to help you make a good choice. *Goodbye Tessa* is a good choice for children reading at White Band in their classroom to read independently.

The aim of independent reading is to read this book with ease, so that your child enjoys the story and relates it to their own experiences.

About the book

Leo and his dog Tessa are inseparable. But one day, Tessa does not come to wake up Leo in his bed as usual. Leo knows something is wrong. Poor Tessa is getting old. Then, one day, she passes away.
How will Leo get over the loss – maybe her puppies can help?

Before reading

Help your child to learn how to make good choices by asking:
"Why did you choose this book? Why do you think you will enjoy it?"
Look at the cover together and ask: "Who is the book about? What sort of relationship do you think the boy and the dog have? Why? What else does the title tell you about what might happen in the story?" Remind your child that they can break longer words into syllables or sound out letters to make a word if they get stuck.
Decide together whether your child will read the story independently or read it aloud to you.

During reading

Remind your child of what they know and what they can do independently. If reading aloud, support your child if they hesitate or ask for help by telling the word. If reading to themselves, remind your child that they can come and ask for your help if stuck.

After reading

Support comprehension by asking your child to tell you about the story. Use the story order puzzle to encourage your child to retell the story in the right sequence, in their own words. The correct sequence can be found on the next page.

Help your child think about the messages in the book that go beyond the story and ask: "How does Leo cope with the loss of his pet? What effects does it have on him? How do other people help him?" Give your child a chance to respond to the story: "Why do you think Leo did not want another dog or puppy? Why did he feel sad when Jasper found a new home?"

Extending learning

Help your child reflect on the story and empathise with Leo, by asking: "What would you do if your pet died? Would you get another one? Why /Why not? What made Leo change his mind about having a new pet?"

In the classroom your child's teacher may be looking at predicting what might happen on the basis of what has been read so far. Ask your child to find some clues in the story that indicate Tessa is not well. Ask them why they think it is still a shock to Leo when Tessa dies.

Look at the plot and key events and ask them to pinpoint two or three events that are important and how each one effects what happens next, to reinforce story sequencing.

Franklin Watts
First published in Great Britain in 2018
by The Watts Publishing Group

Copyright © The Watts Publishing Group 2018
All rights reserved.

Series Editors: Jackie Hamley and Melanie Palmer
Series Advisors: Dr Sue Bodman and Glen Franklin
Series Designer: Peter Scoulding

A CIP catalogue record for this book is
available from the British Library.

ISBN 978 1 4451 6276 8 (hbk)
ISBN 978 1 4451 6278 2 (pbk)
ISBN 978 1 4451 6277 5 (library ebook)

Printed in China

Franklin Watts
An imprint of
Hachette Children's Group
Part of The Watts Publishing Group
Carmelite House
50 Victoria Embankment
London EC4Y 0DZ

An Hachette UK Company
www.hachette.co.uk

www.franklinwatts.co.uk

FSC
www.fsc.org
MIX
Paper from
responsible sources
FSC® C104740

Answer to Story order: 5, 4, 1, 2, 3